NICODEMUS BORN AGAIN IN THE 90's

By
Hilda M. Sonnier-Lynch

WESTBOW
PRESS
A DIVISION OF THOMAS NELSON

WestBow Press books may be ordered through booksellers or by contacting:

WestBow Press
A Division of Thomas Nelson
1663 Liberty Drive
Bloomington, IN 47403
www.westbowpress.com
1-(866) 928-1240

Because of the dynamic nature of the Internet, any web addresses or links contained in this book may have changed since publication and may no longer be valid. The views expressed in this work are solely those of the author and do not necessarily reflect the views of the publisher, and the publisher hereby disclaims any responsibility for them.

Any people depicted in stock imagery provided by Thinkstock are models, and such images are being used for illustrative purposes only.

Certain stock imagery © Thinkstock.

ISBN: 978-1-4497-4085-6 (sc)

Library of Congress Control Number: 2012903571

Printed in the United States of America

WestBow Press rev. date: 11/15/2012

COVERANT
THE RAINBOW IN THE SKY

A COVERANT BETWEEN GOD AND ABRAHAM PEOPLE IN THE WORLD.

MATTHEW 6:9-10

After this manner therefore pray ye: Our Father which art in heaven, Hallowed be thy name. Thy kingdom come. Thy will be done on EARTH, as it is in HEAVEN.

SAINT JOHN 3:16-18

For GOD so loved the world, that he gave his only Begotten Son, that whosoever believeth in him should not perish (die), but have everlasting life. For GOD sent not his Son into the world to condemn the world; but that the world through him might be SAVED.

He that believeth on him is not condemned: <u>but he That believeth not is condemned already</u>, because he hath not believed in the name of the only begotten Son of GOD.

PEOPLE IN THE WORLD

<u>I CORINTHIANS 2:9</u>

But it is written, EYE HATH NOT SEEN,

NOR EAR HEARD, NEITHER HAVE

ENTERED INTO THE HEART OF MAN,

THE THINGS WHICH GOD HATH

PREPARED FOR THEM THAT

LOVE HIM.

TABLE OF CONTENTS

PREFACE
I PETER 1:14-23

As obedient children, not fashioning yourselves according to the former lusts in your ignorance. But as he which hath called you is holy, so be ye holy in all manner of conversation.

Because it is written, **BE YE HOLY; FOR I AM HOLY**

And if ye call on the Father, who without respect of persons judgeth according to every man's work, pass the time of your sojourning here in fear. Forasmuch as ye know that ye were not redeemed with corruptible things, as silver and gold, from your vain conversation received by tradition from your fathers.

But with the precious blood of Christ, as of a lamb without blemish and without spot. Who verily was foreordained before the foundation of the world, but was manifest in these last times for you.

Who by him do believe in GOD, that raise him up from the dead, and gave him glory; that your faith and hope might be in GOD. Seeing ye have purified your souls in obeying the truth through the Spirit unto unfeigned love of the brethren, see that ye love one another with a pure heart fervently.

Being born again, not of corruptible seed, but of incorruptible, by the word of GOD, which liveth and abideth forever.

DEDICATION

The book called "Nicodemus Born Again in the 90's" is dedicated to GOD only begotten Son, JESUS of NAZARETH.

SAINT JOHN 1:10-12

He was in the world, and the world was made by him, and the world knew him not. He came unto his own, and his own received him not. But as many as received him, to them gave He power to become the sons of GOD, even to them that believe on his name.

ISAIAH 53:1-5

Who hath believed our report? And to whom is the arm of the LORD revealed?

For he shall grow up before him as a tender plant, and as a root out of a dry ground: he hath no form nor comeliness; and when we shall see him, there is NO BEAUTY that we should desire him.

He is despised and rejected of men; a man of sorrows, and acquainted with grief: and we hid as it were our faces from him; he was despised, and we esteemed him not.

Surely he hath borne our griefs, and carried our sorrows: yet we did esteem him stricken, smitten of GOD, and afflicted.

But he was wounded for our transgressions; he was bruised for our iniquities: the chastisement of our peace was upon him; and with his stripes we are healed.

ISAIAH 53:6-11

All we like sheep have gone astray; we have turned every one to his own way; and the LORD hath laid on him the iniquity of us all. He was oppressed, and he was afflicted, yet he opened not his mouth: he is brought as a lamb to the slaughter, and as a sheep before her shearers is dumb, so he openeth not his mouth.

He was taken from prison and from judgment: and who shall declare his generation? For he was cut off out of the land of the living: for the transgression of my people was he stricken.

And he made his grave with the wicked, and with the rich in his death; because he had done no violence, neither was any deceit in his mouth. Yet it pleased the LORD to bruise him; he hath put him to grief: when thou shalt make his soul an offering for sin, he shall see his seed, he shall prolong his days, and the pleasure of the LORD shall prosper in his hand.

He shall see of the travail of his soul, and shall be satisfied: by his knowledge shall my righteous servant justify many; for he shall bear their iniquities.

ISAIAH 53:12

Therefore will I divide him a portion with the great, and he shall divide the spoil with the strong; because he hath poured out his soul unto death: and he was numbered with the transgressors; and he bare the sin of many, and made intercession for the transgressors.

ACKNOWLEDGMENT
YAHWEH (GOD NAME IN THE HEBREW BIBLE)
THE FATHER =YAHWEH
THE SON =JESUS
THE HOLY GHOST =TEACHER

SAINT JOHN 3:16-21

*For GOD so loved the world, that he gave his only begotten Son, that whosoever believeth in him should not perish **(DIE),** but have everlasting life.*

For GOD sent not his Son into the world to condemn the world; but that the world through him might be saved.

*He that believeth on him **is not condemned**: but he that believeth **not is condemned already**, because he hath not believed in the name of the only begotten Son of GOD.*

*And this is the condemnation, **that light is come into the world**, and men loved darkness rather than light, because their deeds were evil.*

*For every one that doeth evil **hateth the light**, neither **cometh to the light**, lest his deeds should be reproved.*

But he that doeth truth cometh to the light, that his deeds may be made manifest, that they are wrought in GOD.

REVELATION 4:11

Thou are worthy, O LORD, to receive glory and, honor and power: For thou hast created all things, and for thy pleasure they are and were created.

(NOT HILDA'S PLEASURES; who did lie to my mind that it was ok to have my cake and eat it to? ...P-A-R-T-Y)

GALATIANS 5:7-8

Ye did run well; who did hinder you that ye should not obey the truth? This persuasion cometh not of Him that calleth you.

GENESIS 1:1-2

In the beginning GOD created the heaven and the earth. And the earth was without form, or void; and darkness was upon the face of the deep. And the Spirit of GOD moved upon the face of the waters.

SAINTJOHN 1:1-5

In the beginning was the Word, and the Word was with GOD, and the Word was GOD. The same was in the beginning with GOD. All things were made by him; and without him was not anything made that was made.

In him was life; and the life was the light of men. And the light shineth in darkness; and the darkness comprehended it not.

FOREWORD

ROMANS 10:13

FOR WHOSOEVER SHALL CALL UPON THE NAME OF THE LORD SHALL BE SAVED.....

ROMANS 10:14-15

How then shall they call on him in whom they have not believed?

And how shall they believe in him of whom they have not heard?

And how shall they hear without a preacher?

And how shall they preach, except they be sent?

As it is written, How beautiful are the feet of them that preach the gospel of peace, and bring glad tidings of good things!

INTRODUCTION

SAINT JOHN 3:1-21

SAINT JOHN 3:1-7

There was a man of the Pharisees, named **NICODEMUS**, a ruler of the Jews: The same came to JESUS by night, and said unto him, Rabbi, we know that thou are a teacher come from GOD: for no man can do these miracles that thou doest, except GOD be with him.

JESUS answered and said unto him. *Verily, verily, I say unto thee, Except a man be born again, he cannot see the kingdom of GOD.*

NICODEMUS saith unto him, How can a man be born when he is old? Can he enter the <u>second time</u> into his mother's womb, and be born?

JESUS answered, *Verily, verily, I say unto thee, Except a man be born of water and of the Spirit, he cannot enter into the kingdom of GOD.*

That which is born of the flesh is flesh; and that which is born of the Spirit is spirit. Marvel not that I said unto thee, Ye must be born again.

SAINT JOHN 3:8-15

The wind bloweth where it listeth, and thou hearest the sound thereof, but canst not tell whence it cometh, and whither it goeth; so is every one that is born of the Spirit.

NICODEMUS answered and said unto him, How can these things be?

JESUS answered and said unto him, *Art thou a master of Israel, and knowest not these things? Verily, verily, I say unto thee, We speak that we do know, and testify that we have seen; and ye receive not our witness.*

If I have told you earthly things, and ye believe not, how shall ye believe, if I tell you of heavenly things?

And no man hath ascended up to heaven, but he that came down from heaven, even the Son of man which is in heaven.

And as Moses lifted up the serpent in the wilderness, even so must the Son of man be lifted up: That whosoever believeth in him should not perish, but have eternal life.

AUTHOR BIOGRAPHY

Evangelist Hilda (Clark) Sonnier, 1994
Nickname: **"Nicodemus"**

LUKE 4:18
*THE SPIRIT OF THE LORD IS UPON ME, BECAUSE
HE HATH ANOINTED ME TO PREACH THE GOSPEL
TO THE POOR; HE HATH SENT ME TO HEAL THE
BROKENHEARTED, TO PREACH DELIVERANCE TO
THE CAPTIVES, AND RECOVERING OF SIGHT TO
THE BLIND, TO SET AT LIBERTY THEM THAT ARE
BRUISED,*

*TO PREACH THE ACCEPTABLE YEAR OF THE
LORD.*

JEREMIAH 8:20

The harvest is past,
the summer is ended
and we are not saved.

NICODEMUS
A BORN AGAIN CHRISTIAN IN THE 90'S

JEREMIAH 31:22

How long wilt thou go about, O thou backsliding daughter? For the LORD hath created a new thing in the earth. A woman shall lead a man.

ISAIAH 52:7

How beautiful upon the mountains are the feet of him that bringeth good tidings, that publisheth peace; that bringeth good tidings of good, that publisheth salvation; that saith unto Zion, thy GOD reigneth!

JEREMIAH 3:15

And I will give you pastors according to mine heart, which shall feed you with knowledge and understanding.
(Who said you had to have a church building to be a pastor?)

SAINT JOHN 10:1-2

Verily, verily, I say unto you, He that entereth not by the door into the sheepfold, but climbeth up some other way, the same is a thief and a robber.
But he that entereth in by the door is the SHEPHERD (**PASTOR**) of the sheep. (**JESUS people**)

NICODEMUS BORN AGAIN IN THE 90's

The author, Pastor Hilda Lynch is crying aloud and sparing not, to show the people that is living in the 1900 century their transgressions, and sins. To refresh their thoughts that the GOD we serve is the same yesterday, and today, and forever.

2 PETER 2:4-7
For if GOD spared not the angels that sinned, but cast them down to hell, and delivered them into chains of darkness, to be reserved unto judgment. And spared not the old world, but saved Noah the eighth person, a preacher of righteousness, bringing in the flood upon the world of the ungodly. And turning the cities of Sodom and Gomorrha into ashes condemned them with an overthrow, making them an example unto those that after should live ungodly. And delivered just Lot, vexed with the filthy conversation (cursing/profane words) of the wicked.

The book "Nicodemus Born Again In The 90's" reveals the truth and nothing but the truth about hidden biblical stories and scriptures not preached nor taught in church congregations for years.

The author has researched and found all of her wicked ways she was committing in the King James Bible. She now desires to share her pass dysfunctional wicked ways with readers of "Nicodemus Born Again In The 90's. The book "Nicodemus Born Again In The 90's" is designed to educate families burden with dysfunctional siblings, family and friends living in the 19th century A.D. (After the Death of JESUS through 1900).

The book Nicodemus Born Again In The 90's is written for those who are sick and need to be **RESTORED** from a broken-heart, alcohol, drugs, bondage, incarceration (home/prison/jail/and job) plagues (disease), low self-esteem, unemployed, families abuse, mad at GOD, parent abuse, homeless and children that hate parents.

The book Nicodemus Born Again In The 90's can be used as a day to day family guideline for raising children with good ethic and morals. The 1900 A.D. study guideline book reveals true knowledge of multi-dysfunctional life styles. And reveals warnings that put people souls in jeopardy and the penalties one must suffer for having a rebellious and disobedient spirit toward GOD only begotten Son JESUS.

The information written in the book will help **RESTORE** adult family and friends minds whose wicked ways have not changed.

The author further acknowledge that living in the 1900 A.D. century as an American she had to pray to the LORD for wisdom and understand. It was very important to her to get her own house inside of her body in order.

NICODEMUS BORN AGAIN IN THE 90's

The author acknowledge that she do not know GOD thoughts neither this ways-ISAIAH 55:8; and that her righteousness is as filthy rags before the LORD -ISAIAH 64:6; and that she herself have sinned and come short of the glory of GOD-ROMAN 3:23

And with that in mind she study the Holy Bible daily and it became the best daily guideline to correct her wicked ways. She was able to start recognizing her sins that she was committing.

The author became a hearer of the word of GOD; and then a believer of the word of GOD. The more she study the word of GOD the more she became a doer of the word of GOD. For twenty years the author has press toward the mark for the high calling of GOD in CHRIST JESUS - PHILIPPIANS 3:14.

Yes, I acknowledge GOD only begotten Son name JESUS. And I lift JESUS up daily; because I know I cannot get to GOD except through His only begotten Son JESUS.

I have been blessed with a second time with a second chance in life. My joy has returned to me and my health. Even living in a bad economic crisis my dry bones is LIVING again and LAUGHING and LOVING my sisters and brothers in JESUS name. Thou my necessities are upon me now, I look to the future of becoming successful and prosperous.

NICODEMUS BORN AGAIN IN THE 90's

The book Nicodemus Born Again In The 90's will also educate children about their parents dysfunctional life styles. Parents are human to and their children need to know that their tribulations were assigned to them on earth by **JESUS** before he ascended on high. Parents still have gifts and blessings for their children.

Parent can speak blessings or curses into their children life. Hilda Sonnier father J.D. Clark –Galveston, Texas a Veteran of WWII suffered from mental and alcohol problems because of the war. It was Hilda's alcohol daddy help put her back on the right track of her assigned predestination path, he nick-named her **Nicodemus**.

All glory and honor to JESUS CHRIST of NAZARETH for using my alcoholic daddy J.D. "Geese" Clark , whom I loved very much. He placed me with good parents with love for me and in a good environment.

Pastor Hilda Lynch desire readers to know it is not too late to do the work of an evangelist and endure afflictions until the end and to work JESUS CHRIST OF NAZARETH MINISTRY.

Readers of "Nicodemus Born Again In The 90's need to understand the second water immersion baptism, and the purpose for being baptized in the name of JESUS.

John the Baptist went into all the countries about Jordan, preaching the baptism of repentance for the remission of sins. John the Baptist baptized JESUS the second time LUKE 3:21, we also must be baptized again. John the Baptist baptized the people with water, but JESUS disciples baptized the people with the Holy Ghost and with fire LUKE 3:16.

1 CORINTHIANS 10:1-12

Moreover, brethren, I would not that ye should be **IGNORANT**, how that all our fathers were under the cloud, and all passed through the sea.

And were all **BAPTIZED UNTO MOSES** in the cloud and in the sea. And did all eat the same spiritual meat. And did all drink the same spiritual drink: for they drank of that spiritual Rock that followed them: that Rock was CHRIST.

But with many of them **GOD WAS NOT WELL PLEASED**: for they were overthrown in the wilderness. Now these things were our examples, to the intent we should not lust after evil things, as they also lusted.

I TIMOTHY 6:6-8

But godliness with contentment is great gain. For we brought nothing into this world, and it is certain we can carry nothing out.

And having **FOOD** and **CLOTHES** let us be therewith **CONTENT**.

Evangelist Hilda M. Sonnier, Chaplain

-Texas Baptist Volunteer Chaplain, 1995 License

-Texas Department Of Criminal Justices, 1995 –Volunteer Chaplain

**-GOD TEMPLE FOR DELIVERANCE MINISTRY
TEXAS, 1994
TEXAS, 1998 -**501C)(3) non-denominational, non-profit, tax- exempt, LOVE organization. Strengthen the hands of the poor and the needy.

B.A.D.S. -Biblical/Alcohol/Drugs/Smoking Chemical Dependency

**MS. HILDA'S SOUL FOOD BIBLE STUDY
(Inmates and family members)**

OBEDIENT TO JESUS CHRIST OF NAZARETH GOSPEL

MARK 14:1-9   A WOMAN MEMORIAL

And being in Bethany in the house of Si'mon the leper, as he sat at meat, there came A WOMAN having an alabaster box of ointment of spikenard very precious; and she brake the box, and poured it on his head.

And there were some that had indignation within themselves, and said, Why was this waste of the ointment made? For it might have been sold for more than three hundred pence, and have been given to the poor. And they murmured against her.

And JESUS said, Let her alone; why trouble ye her? She hath wrought a good work on me. For ye have the poor with you always, and when-so-ever ye will ye may do them good: but me ye have not always. She hath done what she could: she is come aforehand to anoint my body to the burying.

Verily I say unto you, Wheresoever this gospel (JESUS GOSPEL) shall be preached throughout the whole world, this also that she hath done shall be spoken of for a MEMORIAL OF HER.

SAINT JOHN 11:1-2

Now a certain man was sick, named Lazarus, of Beth'any, the town of Mary and her sister Martha. (It was that MARY which anointed the LORD with ointment, and wipe his feet with her hair, whose brother Lazarus was sick.

I SAMUEL 15:22-23

To obey is better than sacrifice, and to hearken than the fat of rams. For rebellion is as the sin of witchcraft, and stubbornness is as iniquity and idolatry.

Because thou hast rejected the word of the LORD, he hath also rejected thee from being king.

PART 1
WELCOME
TODAY'S WORLD IS
BUSINESS AS USUAL

JEREMIAH 2:21
Yet I had planted thee a noble vine, wholly a right seed (SHEEP). How then are thou turned into the degenerate plant of a strange vine (GOATS) unto me GOD?

WELCOME
IT IS TESTIMONY TIME
…tell the truth, shut the devil mouth and lock his jaws.
Now we all know that we will not tell our true testimonies
unless we have really renounced Satan and his evil deeds.
A testimony is not just praising the LORD nor just thanking
the LORD. But telling exactly what sins the LORD deliver
you from.

ROMANS 3:23
Now we have all sinned and came short to the glory of
GOD.

ISAIAH 64:6
But we are all as an unclean thing, and all our righteousness
are as fifty rags.

The question is what has GOD deliver you from? If you
never go through anything, GOD cannot deliver you out of
anything.

And for sure the devil will always visit you because he
knows you are trying very hard to keep you evil deeds a
secret. The devil wait for the perfect time to expose your
evil deeds (parties, co-workers, church congregation,
Elections: City, State, White House, Doctor offices etc.)

SAINT LUKE 12:2-3

For there is nothing covered, that shall not be revealed; neither hid, that shall not be known.

Therefore whatsoever ye have spoken in darkness shall be heard in the light; and that which ye have spoken in the ear in closets shall be proclaimed upon the housetops.

JEREMIAH 2:19

Thine own wickedness shall correct thee, and thy backslidings shall reprove thee: know therefore and see that it is an evil thing and bitter, that thou forsaken the LORD thy GOD, and that my fear is not in thee, saith the LORD GOD of hosts.

JEREMIAH 2:20

For of old time I have broken thy yoke, and burst thy bands; and thou saidst, I will not transgress; when upon every high hill and under every green tree thou wanderest, playing the harlot.

PSALM 40:1-4

I waited patiently for the LORD: and he inclined unto me, and heard my cry. He brought me up also out of a horrible pit, out of the miry clay, and set my feet upon a rock, and established my goings.

And he hath put a new song in my mouth, even praise unto our GOD: many shall see it, and fear, and shall trust in the LORD.

Blessed is that man that maketh the LORD his trust, and respecteth not the proud, nor such as turn aside to lies.

HILDA'S BIRTH TESTIMONY

EZEKIEL 16:4
And as for thy nativity, in the day thou wast born thy navel was not cut, neither wast thou washed in water to supple thee; thou wast not salted at all, nor swaddled at all.

HILDA'S BIRTH TESTIMONY

Little Hilda's daddy J.D. Clark was a very dysfunctional man. He was an alcoholic who killed civilians by reason of military mental problems. At Hilda's birth J.D. was in jail and he scream through the old jail window to a friend, name it **NICODEMUS.**

J.D. mother who name was Hilda had ask J.D. to raise his next new born child. Being a girl baby she name her little Hilda. It was then that little Hilda was nickname by her daddy **NICODEMUS.**

Now the nickname **NICODEMUS** did not mean for Little Hilda to become a package deal for the Gay life style (Homosexuality); but to help guide her toward her predestination. When Hilda got to her end and became tired of being tried and deceived with sinful acts. The nickname **NICODEMUS** began to trouble her spirit until she research the Holy Bible scripture concerning the life style of **NICODEMUS.**

Studying the story about **NICODEMUS** little Hilda spirit rested, it was like a burden had been lifted off of her. Off and on Little Hilda's spirit would still trouble her and she knew she had to read the Holy Bible more and meditate to the LORD about her sinful ways and her nickname **NICODEMUS.**

Then I had memories about Big Hilda's home training and how she raised me up in church. Big Hilda did not believe in church mess that cause hurt and ran people away from church, school mess that hurt students and cause them to drop-out, job mess that hurt people and cause them to quick a good paying job, etc. Big Hilda was out spoken and straight forward.

Big Hilda loved Little Hilda; but Little Hilda would not receive Big Hilda love as she grew older. The fact being Big Hilda was not little Hilda's real parent and the real parents had given her away.

Now Little Hilda never saw Big Hilda drinking strong drinks, smoking or even heard of her going out to night clubs. She did however; know that Big Hilda would sit in her kitchen window looking out praying and talking with the LORD. Thank GOD.

Little Hilda still rebel against Big Hilda (against GOD who had given her a good home to be cared for) and Little Hilda could not wait to leave home. Yes, J.D. Clark gave Little Hilda to his mother Big Hilda to love. Little Hilda was raised up in church. Little Hilda never stopped going to church even when she was going through her tribulations.

Today in 2009 Little Hilda is still in church wherever she resided.

PROVERBS 22:6
Train up a child in the way he should go: and when he is old, he will not depart from it.

HILDA'S SCHOOL TESTIMONY

2 TIMOTHY 2:15
Study to shew thyself approved unto GOD, a workman that needeth not to be ashamed, rightly dividing the word of truth.

HILDA'S SCHOOL TESTIMONY

Hilda's attitude was really bad as a child, causing her to be miserable day after day. Her miserable attitude that attack her mind made her school days her worst nightmare.

Hilda was a very dysfunctional student at school and believed in cursing, fighting and was rebellious against the teachers. As time went on Hilda had to be counsel for her action at school and was suspended from school a number of times. Hilda finally decided to settle down and tried to learn all that she could.... But w**as it too late?**

The Devil Never Forgets And Never Forgives.
Rev. Sublet –Huntsville, Texas

Hilda attended school for twelve years and three weeks before graduation the counselor told Hilda she would not graduate because she was short (½) credit.

This is called Teachers Payback v.s. B.A.D. Hilda became discourage and quick school for being a half (½) credit short.

Was it too late? Yes with man....and No with JESUS?

JESUS blood made all things new again to forget and forgive.

JESUS blood paid Satan price IN FULL for our souls.

WE...! The people of the world were purchased with the BLOOD of JESUS not money nor silver or gold.

...so, what's up with the MONEY/OIL/DRUGS/WARS?
fighting, arguing and killing = long sentencing for prisoners

Know that we are owned by GOD's only begotten Son JESUS the prophet of NAZARETH of Galilee -MATTHEW 21:11.

JESUS the high priest who has pasted into the heaven and is seated at the right hand side of His Father; GOD who is the Father of Abraham, Isaac and Jacob our 3-forefathers
THAT'S RIGHT OUR SOULS WERE NOT REDEEMED WITH CORRUPTIBLE THINGS, AS SILVER AND GOLD, FROM YOUR VAIN CONVERSATION RECEIVED BY TRADITION FROM YOUR FATHERS; (MOSES DAYS AND BAPTISM). Moses teaching is still good.

SAINT LUKE 24:44
And he said unto them, *These are the words which*
I spake unto you, while I was yet with you, that all
things must be fulfilled, which were written in the
law of Moses, and in the prophets, and in psalms,
concerning me.

"Shut the devil mouth and lock his jaws"
In memory of -Apostle Mary Smith –a woman of GOD
LaMarque, Texas and West Texas City, Texas.

MARRIAGE –FROM GOOD TO BAD

ECCESIASTES 4:9-12
Two are better than one; because they have a good reward for their labour. For if they fall, the one will lift up his fellow: but woe to him that is alone when he falleth; for he hath not another to help him up.

Again, if two lie together, then they have heat: but how can one be warm alone? And if one prevail against him, two shall withstand him; and a threefold cord (JESUS) is not quickly broken.

NICODEMUS BORN AGAIN IN THE 90's

Being a prominent married woman with three beautiful daughters and having a good paying job at a chemical plant. I enjoyed two cigarettes per day; one cigarette to work and one cigarette going home.

My husband was a young handsome high yellow man. He was young and foolish like me; he was never taught to love himself, just work construction and drink beer; so how could he love me? He started a family outside the home.

Then my marriage turn bad and I was so hurt... this is called true PAIN. Please understand that marriage pain and affliction (sickness/illness) pain are different. It felt like a part of my body had left me.

After my husband started a new family outside the home we would fight and argue daily growing farther apart. It was so hard to keep that big yellow handsome man at home. Frogs (ladies) came out of the ponds, pools, lakes and the wood works and hop away with him.

I began to shoot at him to keep him from entering the home. It was then that I realized I had to separate from him or the three brothers Lucifer/ Satan /Devil; would make me kill him. I did not want to live, I did not want to die, I did not want to kill myself, I did not want to kill my husband, I did not want to kill my children, nor did I want to KILL ....ANYONE (EXODUS 20:15 COMMANDMENT-THOU SHALL NOT KILL

I just wanted to get an old time slavery razor stripe and beat his ?..?..?   But I had a forgiving heart and got my divorce and started a new life for me and my children. I had to live; I had three children that love me and depended on me to care for them. I needed to live and share my love with them.

JESUS did not have to speak the word ?..?.? (He rode it to town and all walked behind it O.K.

HILDA'S WORK TESTIMONY

I THESSALONIANS 4:11-12
And that ye study to <u>be quite</u>, and to do <u>your own business</u>, and to <u>work with your own hands</u> as we commanded you; That ye may <u>walk honestly</u> toward them that are without, and that <u>YE MAY HAVE LACK OF NOTHING</u>.

WISE THOUGHT FOR TODAY!
.....I DO NOT OWN A BELT ...
.....IGOT TO WALK AND USE MY HANDS TO HOLD MY PANTS UP
....I GOT TO USE MY HANDS TO PICK UP MY DOG POOP AND PUT IN A BAG AND THEN USE MY HANDS TO PACK THE BAG OF POOP TO THE NEAREST TRASH BIN....

I DO NOT HAVE TIME TO FARM WITH MY HANDS OR MARKET MY EATABLE PRODUCTS TO BECOME SUCCESSFUL AND PROSPEROUS.

I AM BUSINESS USING MY HANDS TO..........

GREEN AREAS ...?
FARMERS BROWN ....?
WHAT HAPPEN TO MY MULE AND MY LAND?
WHAT HAPPEN TO MY SILVER AND MY GOLD?

HILDA'S WORK TESTIMONY

Hilda worked as a Cook at many different restaurants in Texas, Ramada Inn, Holiday Inn, Anna Bell Restaurant and several others.

Hilda graduated from the Houston Texas School Of Nursing and work for the Nurses Registry at St. Mary Hospital and Mainland Hospital, Nursing Homes and Convalescent Facilities.

Hilda worked for Emmett Lowery Construction for three (3) years located at Union Carbide Plant in Texas City, Texas.

In June, 1976 Hilda was hired for Union Carbide Chemical Plant in Texas City, Texas. Hilda's accepted all jobs offer to her at the plant. The different jobs gave Hilda the opportunity to learn on hand experience as a Security Guards, Reproduction Clerk, Mail Clerk and last of all Engineering Clerk. Hilda retired from Union Carbide Chemical Plant after twenty (20) years of service.

Hilda enrolled in many non-credit classes at work and at the College Of Mainland –Texas City, Texas to help her maintain different jobs skills. Classes –Mechanical Engineering, Business Division, Communication Skills, Small Business for entrepreneurs.

Was it too late to graduate with JESUS? No
What the devil meant for bad JESUS BLOOD turned it to good. Thanks be to JESUS OF NAZARETH. Yes, JESUS LOVES HILDA.

HILDA'S STEALING TESTIMONY

EXODUS 20: 15
THOU SHALT NOT STEAL

HILDA STEALING TESTIMONY

When Hilda became an adult and got marry she started stealing to make ends meet at home. This was another trick of the devil. The town people would whisper behind Hilda back that she could steal Baking Powder out of a bake cake.

The people never stopped to thank Hilda for keeping their families fed month after month. The neighborhood home freezers was so full of food. They could not put one pack of wieners in it and yet they never called to say thank you.

Stealing cause Hilda to have so many friends; she felt like she was in competition with the first lady at the White House. But the good old days soon ran out and Hilda started going to jail she was like a black sheep sitting in the middle of a big brown prairie along.

Little Hilda's grandmother Big Hilda, always taught little Hilda about people who did not have a high school education; a brutish man that have not the understanding of a man. One who never learned wisdom, nor have the knowledge of the HOLY.

GOD allowed Big Hilda to live a long successful and prosperous life -1900-1984. With her on hand experience she believed that if an out of controlled dysfunctional person did not have wisdom, high school education and wanted to do it their way.

All they had to do was stand on the corner with slothful (lazy) people; homeless or living in shelters (looking for freebies). In thirty seconds you can learn more in one day than a college graduate in two years and become awarded with your own License Certificate with a BS Degree.

Oh yes Big Hilda was right, I was sentence to prison for three (3) year(s) for stealing, the judge was merciful to dumb little Hilda and gave her one year good behavior on probation.

I was released from probation with one year good behavior and I retired from stealing. I do not want anything that belong to someone else; including freebies. These was the good old days when Jail and Prison sentencing was not an Evil Business for man $$$gain.

I REPENTED FOR MY EVIL DEEDS AND STOPPED STEALING.

Big Hilda said when a person became fifty (50) years old, if he/she did not have it; most likely they would not get it.

THE NUMBER **50** STAND FOR **PENTICOST**

Today in the year of 2009 Jail and Prison sentencing start at ten (10-25) years and billions of dollars are invested into the system. The devil got it going on.

There will never be enough money to build prison and jail facilities. I think more Nursing Homes need to be built and bars put on the windows.

1 JOHN 4:20
If a man say, I love GOD and hateth his brother, he is a liar: for he that loveth not his brother whom he hath seen, how can he love GOD whom he hath not seen?

ISAIAH 42:22   <u>HID IN PRISON HOUSES</u>
But this is a people robbed and spoiled; they are all of them snared in holes, and they are hid in prison houses: they are for a prey, and none delivereth; for a spoil, and none saith, RESTORE.

HILDA'S ALCOHOL TESTIMONY

HABAKKUK 2:14
WOE unto him that giveth his neighbour drink, that puttest thy bottle to him, and makest him drunken also that thou mayest look on their nakedness!

HILDA'S ALCOHOL TESTIMONY

Hilda started drinking at a young age, about twelve. I can
remember my aunt Bessie coming to live with us. She was
a prominent woman and loved her Gin. One day I
discovered that she had Breast Cancer and her bandages
had to be change often. I watch her drink some of
her Gin before changing her breast bandage.

One day she asked me if I was going to help her. I replied
if you give me some of your Gin I will help you. Aunt
Bessie said well I need some help so I will give you a taste.
Aunt Bessie turned her bottle up and than gave me a taste.
She asked me if I like it and I said… y e s.

I told aunt Bessie I would be her nurse and help with her
bandage for a taste of her Gin. Aunt Bessie passed away
the next week and that good old Gin taste with it.

Hilda got marry and began to drink sociable and when she
started working she would stop on the way home from
work and have a sociable drink. As time went on and peer
pressure got to Hilda she began to drink even more.

This went on until the night that she got so intoxicated and
woke up sitting in a pale of water. Hilda thought to herself
"Girl you know you got it going on" and went to bed.

Thank GOD for sending Hilda's brother Elderly Franklin R. Clark home, 11-6-49 to 12-08-1994. Hilda followed her brother Elderly Franklin R. Clark to church the week of her birthday and he prayed for her by laying his hands on her head with Olive Oil. GOD honor his prays for Hilda that Sunday in church and stopped Hilda cold turkey overnight from drinking and smoking (1994-2009).

NICODEMUS BORN AGAIN IN THE 90's

Many days had past Hilda's birthday before she realized she was not drinking nor smoking cigarettes and the good thing about it was. Hilda no longer wanted to drink or smoked cigarettes. Thanks for the BLOOD of JESUS.

Today, Hilda still work as an evangelist in different communities streets with people who drink and smoke. And her desires to smoke or drink strong drinks are not present.

I never wanted to receive JESUS as my personal savior because I wanted to P-A-R-T-Y. I love to drink that MD and Thunderbird wine with strawberry pop, Jack Daniel, Seagram Gin, Lone Star Beer: you name it and I l-o-v-e it. And dance the night away PARTY.

My neighbors and associates had the nerves to ask me if GOD really call me to be an evangelist. I told them the only reason why they were still drinking strong drinks and beer was because GOD stop me. I was not trying to leave them any thing to drink for a social life style or experience the life style of an alcoholic.

Hilda is still sober and do not drink or smoke cigarettes.
1994-2009
Hilda is now celebrating fifteen (15) years SOBIETY, NON SMOKER and HOLY GHOST FILLED. Thanks to GOD ONLY BEGOTTEN SON JESUS CHRIST OF NAZARETH LOVE.

Hilda received a Deliverance and <u>Rereward</u> from JESUS CHRIST OF NAZARETH BLOOD SALVATION for his bruises, wounds and stripes.

Hilda is praising JESUS all her remaining days of her life, Hallelujah.

PSALM 16:8
Hilda is setting the LORD before her: because He is the shade upon her right hand. Hilda shall not be MOVED.

HILDA'S SMOKING TESTIMONY

ISAIAH 42:1-3
Behold my servant, whom I uphold; mine elect, in whom my soul delighteth; I have put my spirit upon him: he shall bring forth judgment to the Gentiles.

He shall not cry, nor lift up, nor cause his voice to be heard in the street. A bruised reed shall he not break; and the smoking flax shall he not quench: he shall bring forth judgment unto truth.

HILDA'S SMOKING TESTIMONY

Being a prominent married woman with three beautiful daughters and having a good paying job at a chemical plant. I enjoyed two cigarettes per day; one cigarette to work and one cigarette returning home.

Living in with an abusive marriage so great; my mind no longer function properly to have self-control in my life. Yes, I made it to a ½ pack per.

Cigarettes became a thing of the day. I paid a high dollar to inhale dung. Nothing from nothing leaves nothing; but smoking cigarettes you get LUND CANCER= COPD.

I was paying the Cigarette Factory to kill me; JESUS had mercy on my rebellious spirit toward Him and stop me from smoking.

REPROBATED MIND FROM GOD

DEUTERONOMY 28:28
The LORD shall smite thee with madness, and blindness, and astonishment of heart.

ROMANS 1:26-32
For this cause GOD gave them up unto vile affections: For even their women did change the natural use into that which is against nature: And likewise also the men, leaving the natural use of the woman, burned in their lust one toward another; men with men working that which is unseemly, and receiving in themselves that recompence of their error which was meet.

And even as they did not like to retain GOD in their knowledge, **GOD gave them over to a reprobate mind, to do those things which are not convenient;** Being filled with all unrighteousness, fornication, wickedness, covetousness, maliciousness; full of envy, murder, debate, deceit, malignity; whisperers, backbiters, haters of GOD, despiteful, proud, boasters, inventors of evil things, **disobedient to parents.**

Without understanding, covenant breakers, without natural affection, implacable, unmerciful: Who knowing the judgment of GOD, that they which commit such things are worthy of death, not only do the same, but have pleasure in them that do them.

Then my marriage turned bad and me with it. Started my whoredom and to top off everything else, I came out of the closet as a Gay playmate. I was not born a Gay person nor the slang words used (Dike/Lesbian) but had that male and female JEZEBEL SPIRIT as the season people in the church congregation that have no sins call it. Hurt had set in and girls love to have fun. I was always shameful of my sinful acts and when I came out of the closet as a Gay (homosexual) and fear came with it.

Yes the fear of GOD was upon me and. The devil LAUGH but he TREMBLE to.

My mind began to play tricks on me and I would see toys crawling toward me, hearing many voices speaking to me at the same time and books jumping off the bookshelf toward me. An Evil Spirits from GOD was attacking my mind and it was called "REPROBATED MIND".

DEUTERONOMY 32:39
See now that I GOD, even I GOD am he, and there is no god with me: I GOD kill, and I GOD make alive; I GOD wound, and I GOD heal; neither is there any that can deliver out of my hand.

1 SAMUEL 16:14
But the Spirit of the LORD departed from Saul, and an evil spirit from the LORD trouble him.

JUDGES 9:23
Then GOD send an evil spirit between Abimelech and the men of Shechem; and the men of Shechem dealt treacherously with Abimelech.

NICODEMUS BORN AGAIN IN THE 90's

I was losing my figure I was not shaped like a brick house
no more and I became pot gutted, flat buttock, bald headed
and looked like a California Raisin.

My beautiful long black hair was gone and I was bald
headed. Why?

MY SINS.

A woman is not to be bald headed like a man. A woman
hair is a glory to her and my glory was gone.

I CORINTHIANS 11:15–
But if a woman have long hair, it is a glory to her: for her
hair is given her for a covering.

HILDA'S PLAGUES TESTIMONY

LEVITICUS 13:18
The flesh also, in which, even in the skin thereof, was a boil, and is healed.

DEUTERONOMY 28:27
The LORD will smite thee with the botch of Egypt, and with the emerods (hemorrhoid), and with the scab, and with the itch, whereof thou canst not be healed.

PLAGUE

I was schedule for hemorrhoid surgery and the doctors could not find the hole to stop the bleeding. I was receiving blood transfusion to maintain the blood I was losing. After surgery I was weak and the doctor told me she was sorry but could not find the hole to stop the bleeding but; if I was still alive in the morning she would take me back to surgery and try again.

When she left I turn over to the wall and talk with JESUS like Captain Hezekiah did and GOD added fifteen years to his life. Then on my death bed I repented to JESUS for my sins and asked him to come into my life and be my personal savior and save me. I renounce Satan and all his evil works. I surrender all to JESUS and asked GOD in the name of JESUS not to let Satan kill me.

And to give me a second chance in life to do the work of an evangelist and apply His statues and His laws to my life style. That I maybe used to win souls to JESUS OF NAZARETH. I told JESUS if no one else would go send me. And I Hilda Sonnier has been on the battle field of the LORD ever since. Hilda.

2 KINGS 20:1-7
GOD ADDED 15- YRS TO HEZEKIAH LIFE

In those days was Hezekiah sick unto death. And the prophet Isaiah the son of Amoz came to him, and said unto him, Thus said the LORD, Set thine house in order; for thou shalt die, and not live.

Then he turned his face to the wall, and prayed unto the LORD, saying, I beseech thee, O LORD, remember now how I have walked before thee in truth and with a perfect heart, and have done that which is good in thy sight. And Hezekiah wept sore.

And it came to pass, afore Isaiah was gone out into the middle court, that the word of the LORD came to him, saying, Turn again, and tell Hezekiah the captain of my people, Thus saith the LORD, the GOD of David thy father, I have heard thy prayer, I have seen thy tears: behold, I will heal thee: on the third day thou shalt go up unto the house of the LORD.

And I will add unto thy days fifteen years: and I will deliver thee and this city out of the hand of the King of Assyria; and I will defend this city for mine own sake, and for my servant David's sake. And Isaiah said, Take a lump of figs. And they took and laid it on the boil, and he recovered.

HILDA'S HOMOSEXUAL TESTIMONY

HOMOSEXUALITY
ABOMINATION UNTO GOD

ISAIAH 3:9 <u>GAY'S OUT OF THE CLOSET</u>
The show of their countenance doth witness against them; and they declare their sin as Sodom, they hide it not. Woe unto their soul! For they have rewarded evil unto themselves.

"JEZBEL MALE AND FEMALE SPIRIT"
(whoredom / orgies / prostitution /drinking / drugs /stealing /oral sex/ smoking etc.)

As a single mother my new life style, lead me to trouble in the waters. I started whoring around and to really top it off, I came out of the closet as a Gay (Homosexual) Playmate. Not born as a Dike or Lesbian just a playmate.

I started going out to more and more night clubs and hearing the same marriage problems that I walked away from. Now there was this special group of people that looked and acted like they really had it going on and I was gained for that.

I started observing them each time that I went out and it was over-whelming how they treated each other in the public. I thinking, man it's got to be ok for the home team. They waited patiently on each other to arrive, at the club with matching garments, hugging each other, holding hands, constantly touching each other, laughing and talking etc.,

When I inquired about this group of people to different associates they told me that they were called "The Happy Group" is the Gay (Homosexuals) and that they never legally married because of the law. (read about the author vote for Gay Marriage).

That night I prayed to GOD for a mate from the special group. Yes, I was very detailed in my order for a mate.

NICODEMUS BORN AGAIN IN THE 90's

I wanted a stud woman that walked like a stud and worn
Stacy Adam shoes, very clean person who like to bath
daily, dress to occasion for events, clothes press at the
cleaners, jewelry, good housekeeper, traveling partner, no
arguments or fighting, love JESUS with all their heart and
love attending church services.

Hilda did not keep control of her body and allowed herself to become over sex lusting twenty-four seven. It is not enough sex in the world for that, it is more to life than sex. And to think Hilda allowed Homosexuality to enter into her life style from an abusive marriage. To have sex with another woman who had the same sex organs. Thanks for the BLOOD of JESUS.

As a Gay sex partner there was no doubt in my mind about 24/7 loving. Now the **ORAL SEX** was another issue, ok......
......................**WE CANNOT EAT UP TEXAS**!!!!!!!!!!!!!!

In one week it was on....ok. I met Mr. Do Right and I thought to myself...you go girl...P-A-R-T-Y and non stop P-A-R-T-Y till the club close. DID YOU SAY "THANK GOD FOR FRIDAY's (run children run). I SAY THANK JESUS FOR HIS BLOOD

DID I THINK PEOPLE LOVE ME? because they smile and laugh in my face, because they love my cooking, because I party with them, because I work with them?

WELL LISTEN TO THIS.
No one told me that the special group of people life style was an abomination unto GOD? Not one preacher.

Not when I inquired about homosexuality, not before I engaged in homosexuality activity, nor while my relationship was in process, nor after the relationship was over.

The whole community and county knew about my wicked ways. On Sundays I was in church and this is another book).

Pastors and congregation members that knew I was in the relationship talk to me so nice on Sunday's at church and unlimited co-workers in my face. Family members never stop calling and visiting. Thank JESUS for His Blood.

But it was not long before trouble in the waters was choking me. I had been given a "Reprobated Mind" from GOD and the Devil trick me with all of his evil enticing life styles.

I never stop to think about GOD cannot give you what he do not have. So, I was really praying to Lucifer / Devil /Satan. The Anti-Christ is here NOW.

Now it was not just my Reprobated Mind that I was worrying about. I became sicker and had to have several surgeries: Hemorrhage, Hysterectomy, Snake bite, Hernia, Sys, and Gall Bladder.

I thought to myself again; looking for love in all the wrong places again and now I am suffering with **PLAGUES** and have low tolerance for pain.

Doctors hate me when I scream in Emergency Rooms. I try very hard not to go to the hospitals or clinics. I am allergy to:
Morphine
Codeine
Vicodin
Demerol
Penicillin/Sulfa drugs etc.

Now I am free from the homosexual Spirit. And I no longer say RED LOOKS GOOD IN ANY MAN BED. I say RED IS THE BLOOD OF JESUS and I am running for dear life.

Many demons deceived Hilda's **mind** to look for love in all the wrong places. Hilda gave her love, and her **heart** and put her soul in jeopardy for **SEX**. She bonded with an Gay (Homosexuality) unmarried woman not meant for her life style. Today in 2009, Evangelist Hilda Sonnier continue to seek speaking engagement for her testimonies.

We the people must not be non-believers as in Noah days, (THE GREAT WATER FLOOD DESTROYED ALL BUT 8-PEOPLE) but know that Gay (Homosexuality) life style is abomination unto GOD and everyone that practice such deeds will not enter the kingdom of heaven.

DO NOT POINT THE FINGER AT YOUR NEIGHBOR WHICH IS YOUR SISTERS AND BROTHER BY NOAH POPULATIONS THE WORLD......

BUT READ THIS AND EXAMPLE YOURSELF......

PROVERBS 6:16-19
These six (6) things doth the LORD hate: yea, seven (7) are an abomination unto him.

A proud look, a lying tongue, and hands that shed innocent blood, an heart that deviseth wicked imaginations, feet that be swift in running to mischief, a false witness that speaketh lies, and he that soweth discord among brethren.

ORAL SEX

I TIMOTHY 4:8   OVER-SEXED

For bodily exercise (SEX) profiteth little: but godliness is profitable unto all things, having promise of the life that now is, and of that which is to come.

EZEKIEL18:5-9   **ORAL SEX**
EATING UPON THE MOUNTAIN

But if a man be just, and do that which is lawful and right.
<u>And hath not eaten upon the mountains,</u> neither hath lifted
his eyes to the idols of the house of Israel, neither hath
defiled his neighbour's wife, neither hath come near to a
menstruous woman.

And hath not oppressed any,
but hath restored to the debtor his pledge,
hath spoiled none by violence,
hath given his bread to the hungry,
and hath covered the naked with a garment.

He that hath not given forth upon usury (interest),
neither hath taken any increase,
that hath withdrawn his hand from iniquity,
hath executed true judgment between man and man.

Hath walked in my statutes, and hath kept my judgments,
to deal truly; he is just, he shall surely live, saith the LORD
GOD.

PART II

AUTHOR WISDOM

Now many questions began to enter Hilda's mind being over sexed and confused with the "JEZEBEL male and female spirit.

Hilda cried unto the LORD many days concerning her Gay life style. The LORD told Hilda, that He had raised her up with on-hand experience of Homosexuality (Gay life style) to preach the true GOSPEL of JESUS CHRIST OF NAZARETH.

Hilda was chosen by GOD to speak to the nation concerning Homosexuality (Gay Life Style) being an ABOMINATION unto Him. And to reveal several other ABOMINATIONS found in the King James Holy Bible to the nation.

To let the people in the world know that all must turn from their wicked ways and be born again of Spirit and Water

EZEKIEL 18: 21 But if the wicked will turn from all his sins that he hath committed, and keep all my statutes, and do that which is lawful and right, he shall surely live, he shall not die.

2 CHRONICLES 7:14 If my people, which are called by my name, shall humble themselves, and pray, and seek my face, and turn from their wicked ways; then will I hear from heaven, and will forgive their sin, and will heal their land.

The Gay life style (Homosexuality) came through Noah days of populating the world. Noah son Ham the father of the Canaan rape Noah. The door to the "JEZEBEL SPIRIT" was open once again with a welcoming invitation to JESUS people.

NICODEMUS BORN AGAIN IN THE 90's

HOMOSEXUALITY (GAY LIFE STYLE) IS
AN ABOMINATION UNTO GOD.

A REVELATION (PREMONITION) FROM
THE LORD CONCERNING THE HOLY
BIBLE SCRIPTURE -GENESIS 9:20-29.
(THE ANOINTED OLD KING JAMES HOLY BIBLE VERSION)

**85% of the world population
is GAY**

**10% of the world population
is BI-SEXUAL**

**5% of the world population
is HETEROSEXUAL**

To help the people in the world better understand the Ten Commandments of GOD and things that we ONE NATION unto GOD do to displease Him; including ABOMINATION**S** unto GOD.

I research and study the old anointed King James Holy Bible and found many ABOMINATION**S** unto GOD. Now I am able to share with my sisters and brothers in the world a list of those ABOMINATION**S** unto GOD. Not just Gay life style (Homosexuality).

Using the wisdom of GOD, I define how Hilda and her children, grandchildren and great-grandchildren would be classified if we were all true HETEROSEXUAL people. That obeys the commandments of GOD.

PROVERBS 6:16-19
These six (6) things doth the LORD hate: yea, seven (7) are an ABOMINATION unto him.

A PROUD LOOK,

A LYING TONGUE

HANDS THAT SHED INNOCENT BLOOD

AN HEART THAT DEVISETH WICKED IMAGINATIONS

FEET THAT BE SWIFT IN RUNNING TO MISCHIEF

A FALSE WITNESS THAT SPEAKETH LIES.

HE THAT SOWETH DISCORD AMONG BRETHREN

NICODEMUS BORN AGAIN IN THE 90's

These people are my sisters and brothers in JESUS. They were populated through the days of Noah with me. I work with them, they work with me on different jobs and they are my children, grandchildren, great-grandchildren, uncles, aunts, nephews, cousins, daughters and sons.

Why the Gay people marriage cannot enter into the Constitutional Right? The government spends my tax dollars to support their crisis with Food Stamps, Energy Checks, Medicare, Medicaid, Aide and other medical diseases programs they have.

The Gays people are everywhere: government agents, Post office, military, Whitehouse, City and County Officials, Preachers, Lawyers, Doctors, Nurses, Bankers, our night household secret sex pick-up on the corner for (whores, prostitutes, drug addicts, alcoholic, smokers, perverts, peepers, child molesters, rapist, oral sex, pimp etc.

I buy items from Gay people such as: cars, houses, lumber, appliance etc.
I use Gay people Banks and Credit Unions etc.
I even shop at Gay people grocery stores.
I order fast food products from Gay people and they serve us fast food.
I borrow money from Gay people Cash Advance Store. We sell and buy gold from Gay people.
I use Gay people Pawn Shops etc.
I even trade at the Stock Market with Gay people.
And I have the nerves to vote against Gay people right to marry and be registered in our Constitutional Right?

WELL!
WISDOM IS THE PRINCIPAL THING; THEREFORE
GET WISDOM; AND WITH ALL THY GETTING GET
UNDERSTANDING.

CATCH THE ANOINTED VISION OF JESUS.

READ THE SCRIPTURE BELOW FOUND IN THE
NEW TESTAMENT OF THE OLD KING JAMES
HOLY BIBLE.

<u>LUKE 16:8-9</u>

And the LORD commended the unjust steward (sinful, abominations etc.), because he had done wisely: for the children of this world (Satan=darkness) are in their generation wiser than the children of light (JESUS= light).

And I say unto you, Make to yourselves friends of the mammon of unrighteousness; that, when ye fail, they may receive you into everlasting habitations.

I JOHN 4:20-21

IF A MAN SAY, I LOVE GOD, AND HATETH HIS BROTHER, HE IS A LIAR: FOR HE THAT LOVETH NOT HIS BROTHER WHOM HE HATH SEEN, HOW CAN HE LOVE GOD WHOM HE HATH NOT SEEN?

AND THIS COMMANDMENT HAVE WE FROM HIM. THAT HE WHO LOVETH GOD LOVE HIS BROTHER ALSO.

GENESIS 9:20-29

And Noah began to be an husbandman, and he planted a vineyard: And he drank of the wine, and was drunken; and he was uncovered within his tent. And Ham, the father of Canaan, saw the nakedness of his father, and told his two brethren without.

And Shem and Japheth took a garment, and laid it upon both their shoulders, and went backward, and covered the nakedness of their father; and their faces were backward, they saw not their father's nakedness.

And Noah awoke from his wine, and knew what his younger son had done unto him. And he said, Cursed be Canaan; a servant of servants shall he be unto his brethren. And he said, Blessed be the LORD GOD of Shem; and Canaan shall be his servant.

GOD shall enlarge Japheth, and he shall dwell in the tents of Shem; and Canaan shall be his servant. And Noah lived after the flood three hundred and fifty (350) years. And all the days of Noah were nine hundred and fifty (950) years: and he died.

QUESTIONS

HERMAPHRODITE BABIES

I began to think back when I was a girl at home and sit outside the kitchen window to listen to adults conversation about Hermaphrodite babies being born years ago with two different sex organs and the doctors allowed parents to choose between a male or female baby.

Could this have happen to me? GOD I pray big Hilda did not want a baby girl this bad. If she did GOD I forgive her and please I ask you to forgive her for her sins.

-Was I to be a boy baby and was converted to a girl baby?
  (Hermaphrodite babies)
-Was it the LUST of the WORLD that I long to partake in?

LUKE 21:34-36

And take heed to yourselves, lest at any time your hearts be overcharged with surfeiting, and drunkenness, and cares of this life, and so that day come upon you unawares. For as a snare shall it come on all them that dwell on the face of the whole earth. Watch ye therefore, and pray always, that ye may be accounted worthy to escape all these things that shall come to pass, and to stand before the Son of man.

-How did the spirit of Homosexuality return after GOD destroyed the earth?

-Was it because Noah son, Ham "The Father of the Canaan" rape his father Noah when he was drunk.

CONSUMING TO MUCH ALCOHOL
The sky is the limit. REPENT daily.

I am left with so many questions to be answer and Big Hilda past away in 1984. Yet, I pray and seek JESUS CHRIST OF NAZARETH for answers.

I do know one thing for sure; there is no little sin or big sin. Sin is Sin and there is no sin that goes unpaid and I got to get it right fast....Ouch!

NOTHING IS FREE. JESUS PAID A PRICE WITH HIS BLOOD TO WIN OUR SOULS BACK FROM THE DEVIL.

NOTHING WAS FREE! (LUCIFIER)
THERE WAS NO FREEBIES! (SATAN)
AND THE PRICE I PAID THEN AND NOW IN 2011 IS UNBEARABLE (DEVIL)

PSALM 40:1-3
Hilda waited patiently for the LORD; and he inclined unto Hilda, and heard Hilda cry. He brought Hilda up also out of an horrible pit, out of the miry clay, and set Hilda feet upon a rock, and established Hilda goings.

And he hath put a new song in Hilda mouth, even praise unto our GOD: many shall see it and fear, and shall trust in the LORD. Blessed is that man that maketh the LORD his trust, and respecteth not the proud, nor such as turn aside to lies.

NICODEMUS BORN AGAIN IN THE 90's

GENESIS 2:2
And on the seventh day GOD ended his work which he had made; and he rested on the seventh day from all his work which he had made (why do we work on Sundays?)

GENESIS 5:29 And he called his name Noah, saying, This same shall comfort us concerning our work and toil of our hands, because of the ground which the LORD hath cursed.

SAINT JOHN 4:34 Jesus saith unto them, *My meat is to do the will of him that sent me, and to finish his work.*

2011....2011.....2013
CAN YOU TELL YOUR TESTIMONY

BUT THE CHILDREN OF THE KINGDOM SHALL BE CAST OUT INTO OUTER DARKNESS: THERE SHALL BE WEEPING AND GNASHING OF TEETH.

(How have you sinned in GOD eye sight -kill hospital patients, fed people to crocodile, alligators, burned up people, hung people, shot people, cut people, sowed discord among your neighbors,

If your neighbors have REPENTED of their sins and confess their sins before GOD. Are you now talking about them in the public to other people to hid your sins and make you feel safe. Please read Ezekiel 18:22

EZEKIEL 18:22
TALKING ABOUT OTHER PEOPLE TESTIMONIES
All his transgressions that he hath committed, **they shall not be mentioned unto him:** in his righteousness that he hath done he shall live.

Their blood is on your hands. REPENT daily

YOUR BUSINESS IS NOT JUST BETWEEN YOU AND GOD FOR GOD WORD SAY:

JOEL 2:28 And it shall come to pass afterward, that I will pour out my spirit upon all flesh; and your sons and your daughters shall prophesy, your old men shall dream dreams, your young men shall see visions.

LUKE 12:2-3
For there is nothing covered, that shall not be revealed; neither hid, that shall not be known. Therefore whatsoever ye have spoken in darkness shall be heard in the light; and that which ye have spoken in the ear in closets shall be proclaimed upon the housetops.

DO NOT THINK PEOPLE DO NOT KNOW WHAT YOU HAVE DONE. THEY JUST HAVE NOT SAID ANYTHING ....YET. BECAUSE YOU ARE QUICK TO CALL A PERSON CRAZY OR A WITCH. You will want to have them killed or impose medical experiments on them and etc,.

NICODEMUS BORN AGAIN IN THE 90's

Hilda must Repent daily.

Hilda must pray the DISCIPLE PRAY DAILY. MATTHEW 6:9-13 "Our Father"

Hilda have greatly sinned in GOD eye sight,

AS OF 2011 HILDA IS GREATLY ABUSED BY MANY PROFESSIONAL AND NON- PROFESSIONAL PEOPLE.

COULD IT BE HILDA'S SPIRITUAL CALLING. ? God SEE everything we do and HEAR everything we say.

Hilda was DELIVERED and FREED from the Gay life style of Homosexuality Spirit in 1992. Thanks to JESUS CHRIST OF NAZARETH BLOOD.

PART III

HILDA'S MINISTRY WORK

PSALM 68:11
THE LORD GAVE THE WORD: GREAT WAS THE
COMPANY OF THOSE THAT PUBLISHED IT.

HILDA'S MINISTRY WORK

The LORD blessed Hilda with a apostolic calling in 1994. She would remodel and upgrade abandon or to be abandon churches.

The first assigned church was located in La Marque, Texas on Anderson Street. The church was overseen by the woman of GOD -Pastor Virginia Wright.

The second church to be remodel was for Pastor Jackson church in Texas City, Texas and the third church to be remodel was for Apostle Neubine in La Marque, Texas on Hwy 1765. And GOD send pastors after his own heart to conduct church business.

Hilda was invited to join her brother J.D. Hill as a platform guess speaker with the Bill Glass Weekend of Champion Prison Ministry. The ministry flew Hilda and her brother J.D. Hill to different prisons in different states to give their testimonies.

Hilda evangelized daily feeding and ministering the Word of GOD at Beautiful Feet Ministry in Fort Worth, Texas.

AM I my sister keeper?

NICODEMUS DELIVERANCE IN THE 90's
BROTHER -1
EVANGELIST J.D. HILL
STOCKTON, CALIFORNIA

HILDA'S DELIVERANCE

Hilda's "Sin Deliverance" came from GOD, through her brother, J.D. (Clark) Hill at a church revival in Arlington, Texas.

Ministry: CATCH THE VISION MINISTRY
Theme: "Reconciliation"
Guest Speaker: Evangelist J.D. (CLARK) HILL
Buffalo Bills (formerly 5-yrs NFL)

That evening a call came from Hilda's brother J.D. Hill who invited all of his family members in Galveston, Texas to Arlington, Texas.
J.D. asked the family to come and join him in a joyous occasion and to hear him speak. Family members still remember J.D. sermon on Reconciliation.

Many family members attended and it was a great occasion and time for a family reunion.

In 1995 Hilda joined her brother J.D. as a trio sister and brother guest speaker for Bill Glass Weekend of Champion. They evangelized in different state prisons giving their dysfunctional life style testimonies concerning their rise and falls growing up in the 1900's.

Their testimonies were not meant to shame anyone, but to give the people of the kingdom warning about living a sinful life style. And to let the people know that it was not too late to turn from their wicked ways and be RESTORED (SAVED).

Hilda's spirit rejoiced doing the service because many questions that Hilda had, was answer doing her brother sermon in Reconciliation. Hilda no longer wanted to partake in homosexuality.

AM I my sister keeper?

NICODEMUS BORN AGAIN IN THE 90's
BROTHER -2
ELDER FRANKLIN ROOSEVELT CLARK
OAKLAND, CALIFORNIA

ELDER FRANKLIN ROOSEVELT CLARK
I CORINTHIANS 6:10
As sorrowful, yet always rejoicing; as poor, yet making many rich; as having nothing, and yet possessing all things.

HILDA BORN AGAIN IN THE 90's
Hilda's "NEW BIRTH" came in 1993 from GOD, through her brother Elder Franklin R. Clark at the Church Of God In Christ in LaMarque, Texas on Nasby Street.

MALACHI 3:8-12   WILL A MAN ROB GOD?
Will a man rob GOD? Yet ye have robbed me. But ye say, Wherein have we robbed thee? In tithes and offerings.

Ye are curse with a curse: for ye have robbed me, even this whole nation.

Bring ye all the tithes into the storehouse, that there may be meat in mine house, and prove me now herewith, saith the LORD of hosts, if I will not open you the windows of heaven, and pour you out a blessing, that there shall not be room enough to receive it.

And I will rebuke the devourer for your sakes, and he shall not destroy the fruits of your ground, neither shall your vine cast her fruit before the time in the field, saith the LORD of hosts.

And all nations shall call you blessed: for ye shall be a delightsome land, saith the LORD of hosts.

Hilda's brother Elder Franklin Roosevelt Clark of Oakland, California was ill and came home to evangelize his own family members in his last days. He preached at Greater Saint Matthew Church-Pastor Randle -Hitchcock, Texas.

It was at the Church Of God In Christ in LaMarque, Texas on Nasby Street where Hilda followed her brother Franklin to church the week of her birthday and GOD allowed her brother to pray for her salvation Hilda became a born again Christian, ordained, sanctified, and a prophetess unto the nation.

GOD Himself has raised Hilda up as a prophetess unto the nation from a experience Gay life style to give warning to his . Living a GAY (Homosexual) life style is of SATAN MINISTRY....... WARNING GAY LIFE STYLE (HOMOSEXUALITY) IS A ABOMINATION UNTO GOD. REPENT AND SURRENDER ALL TO JESUS.

THE DEVIL LAUGH BUT HE TREMBLE TO!

LET THEM THAT HAVE AN EAR HEAR .....

in JESUS name.

AM I my sister keeper?

NICODEMUS BORN AGAIN IN THE 90's
BROTHER -3
CLEVELAND CLYDE CLARK
LOS ANGLES, CALIFORNIA

CLEVELAND CLYDE CLARK

PSALM 68:6
GOD setteth the solitary in families: he bringeth out those which are bound with chains: but the rebellious dwell in a dry land.

AM I my sister keeper?

NICODEMUS BORN AGAIN IN THE 90's
BROTHER -4
EVANGELIST ALTON EUGENE HAYES

Hilda's brother Alton Eugene Hayes is a great inspiration to her. He is a man of wisdom and love the LORD.

ECCLESIASTES 10:19
A feast is made for laughter, and wine maketh merry: but money answereth all things.

AM I my sister keeper?

NICODEMUS BORN AGAIN IN THE 90's
BROTHER -5
REV. CHESTER SMITH

Hilda's brother Chester Smith started preaching when he was sixteen (16) years old. He is a great inspiration to her. He gave Hilda a scripture to read from the book of:

GALATIANS 5:7
Ye did run well; who did hinder you that ye should not obey the truth?

AM I my sister keeper?

NICODEMUS BORN AGAIN IN THE 90's
BROTHER -6
SYLVESTER CLARK

"ASA LAMA LAKA"

PEACE BE UPON YOU

AM I my wife keeper?

**NICODEMUS A BORN AGAIN CHRISTIAN IN
THE 90's
MY HUSBAND
MITCHELL HENRY LYNCH
JULY 8, 2003**

I CORINTHIANS 1:27
But GOD hath chosen the foolish things of the world to confound the wise. And GOD has chosen the weak things of the world to confound the things which are mighty.

Evangelist Mitchell Lynch and Pastor Hilda Lynch was united in matrimony July 8, 2003 –Galveston, Texas. The marriage is now nine (9) years old and all is well.

Evangelist Mitchell Lynch-62yrs Veteran
US Navy –Honorable discharge
Navy Reserves

Teacher –LaMarque, Tx   Immediate School District
Graduate /Diploma –Winnsboro, Louisiana

WORK HISTORY
Labor Local -116,
Warren Brother Road Construction
Gulf Chemical
Marley Cooling Tower Company
Union Carbide Company
Amoco Chemical Company
Marathon Chemical Company

PART IV
DAILY PRAYERS
AND
SCRIPTURES

REVELATION 12:12

Therefore rejoice, ye heavens, and ye that dwell in them. WOE to the inhabiters of the earth and of the sea!

For the devil is come down unto you, having great wrath (anger), because he knoweth that he hath but a short time.

GOD KNOWS HOW TO DELIVER HIS PEOPLE OUT OF SIN.

2 PETER 2:9
The LORD knoweth how to deliver the godly out of temptations, and to reserve the unjust unto the day of judgment to be punished.

GREATEST COMMANDMENT
Love the LORD thy GOD with all your heart; mind, soul.

Although I repented of my sins and renounce Satan evil works seventeen years ago till today. Necessity and plagues are upon me in 2009.

It is my pray that the book "Nicodemus Born Again in the 90's" will impart in you the same wisdom that it gave me to overcome the devil strongholds.

Yes, I am ordained, sanctified and made holy I can take anything; but everyone needs to be careful for themselves. For JESUS fights Hilda's battles.

JESUS CHRIST OF NAZARETH blood forgave me of my sins, wash me with hyssop and clean me up. Man will never see Hilda as being perfect.

1 PETER 5:10-11

But the GOD of all grace, who hath called us unto his eternal glory by CHRIST JESUS, after that ye have suffered a while, make you perfect, stablish, strengthen, settle you.

To him be glory and dominion forever and ever. AMEN

MATTHEW 6:6-8

But thou, when thou prayest, enter into thy <u>CLOSET</u>, and when thou hast shut thy door, pray to thy Father which is in secret; and thy Father which seeth in secret shall reward thee openly.

But when ye pray, use not vain repetitions, as the heathen do: for they think that they shall be heard for their much speaking. Be not ye therefore like unto them: for your Father knoweth what things ye have need of, before ye ask him.

LORD'S PRAYER
MATTHEW 6:9-13

After this manner therefore pray ye: Our Father which art in heaven, Hallowed be thy name. Thy kingdom come.

Thy will be done in earth, as it is in heaven. Give us this day our daily bread. And forgive us our debts, as we forgive our debtors.

And lead us not into temptation, but deliver us from evil: For thine is the kingdom, and the power, and the glory, for ever. Amen.

THE LORD'S IS MY SHEPHERD

PSALM 23:1-6

The LORD is my shepherd; I shall not want. He maketh me to lie down in green pastures: he leadeth me beside the still waters.

He restoreth my soul: he leadeth me in the paths of righteousness for his name's sake. Yea, though I walk through the valley of the shadow of death, I will fear no evil: for thou art with me; thy rod and thy staff they comfort me.

Thou preparest a table before me in the presence of mine enemies: thou anointest my head with oil; my cup runneth over.

Surely goodness and mercy shall follow me all the days of my life: and I will dwell in the house of the LORD for ever.

PRAYER FOR BLESSING

NUMBERS 6:24-26

The LORD bless thee and keep thee.

The LORD make his face to shine upon thee, and be gracious unto thee.

The LORD lift up his countenance upon thee, and give thee peace.

PRAYER FOR HELP

PSALM 121:1-8

I will lift up my eyes unto the hills, from whence cometh my help. My help cometh from the LORD, which made heaven and earth.

He will not suffer my foot to be moved: he that keepeth thee will not slumber. Behold, he that keepeth Israel will not slumber or sleep.

The LORD is thy keeper: the LORD is thy shade upon thy right hand. The sun shall not smite thee by day, nor the moon by night.

The LORD shall preserve thee from all evil: he shall preserve thy soul. The LORD shall preserve thy going out and thy coming in from this time forth, and even for evermore.

REPENTANCE PRAYER

GOD IN THE NAME OF JESUS I REPENT OF ALL MY SINS. ALL THAT I HAVE SAID, DONE OR EATEN NOT PLEASING IN THY SIGHT.

I RENOUNCE SATAN AND ALL OF HIS EVIL WORKS. I WELCOME JESUS CHRIST OF NAZARETH INTO MY PERSONAL LIFE.

I SURRENDER ALL TO YOU JESUS CHRIST OF NAZARETH. HELP ME TO OVERCOME LUCIFER/SATAN/DEVIL STRONGHOLDS.

HELP ME JESUS CHRIST OF NAZARETH TO DISCERN SATAN MINISTRY AND AVOID HIS EVIL WORKS.

ROMANS 10:9-10

PRAYER FOR SALVATION

THAT IF THOU SHALT CONFESS WITH THY MOUTH THE LORD JESUS, AND SHALT BELIEVE IN THINE HEART THAT GOD HATH RAISED HIM FROM THE DEAD, THOU SHALT BE SAVED.

FOR WITH THE HEART MAN BELIEVETH UNTO RIGHTEOUSNESS; AND WITH THE MOUTH CONFESSION IS MADE UNTO SALVATION.

PROVERBS 4:5-7

PRAY FOR WISDOM

GET WISDOM, GET UNDERSTANDING: FORGET IT NOT; NEITHER DECLINE FROM THE WORDS OF MY MOUTH.

FORSAKE HER NOT, AND SHE SHALL PRESERVE THEE: LOVE HER, AND SHE SHALL KEEP THEE.

WISDOM IS THE PRINCIPAL THINGS; THEREFORE GET WISDOM. AND WITH ALL THY GETTING GET UNDERSTANDING.

PROVERBS 7:1-5

FORSAKE NOT WISDOM

MY SON, KEEP MY WORDS, AND LAY UP MY COMMANDMENTS WITH THEE.

KEEP MY COMMANDMENTS, AND LIVE; AND MY LAW AS THE APPLE OF THINE EYE.

BIND THEM UPON THY FINGERS, WRITE THEM UPON THE TABLE OF THINE HEART.

SAY UNTO WISDOM. THOU ART MY SISTER; AND CALL UNDERSTANDING THY KINSWOMAN.

THAT THEY MAY KEEP THEE FROM THE STRANGE WOMAN, FROM THE STRANGER WHICH FLATTERETH WITH HER WORDS.

PROVERBS 11:29

HE THAT TROUBLETH HIS OWN HOUSE SHALL INHERIT THE WIND: AND THE FOOL SHALL BE SERVANT TO THE WISE OF HEART.

GOD SENT HIS WORD TO HEAL

JOHN 1:1
In the beginning was the WORD, and the WORD was with GOD and the WORD was GOD.

EXODUS 15:26
And said, If thou wilt diligently hearken to the voice of the LORD thy GOD, and wilt do that which is right in his sight, and wilt <u>give ear to his commandments, and keep all his statutes.</u>

I will put none of these diseases upon thee, which I have brought upon the Egyptians: **for I am the LORD that healeth thee.**

EXODUS 23:25
And ye shall serve the LORD your GOD, and He shall bless thy bread (food), and thy water; **and I will take sickness away from the midst of thee.**

PSALM 103:1-3
Bless the LORD, O my soul: and all that is within me, bless his holy name. Bless the LORD, O my soul, and forget not all his benefits: Who forgiveth all thine iniquities; **who healeth ALL thy diseases.**

PSALM 107:20
He sent His word, and healed them, and delivered them from their destructions.

PSALM 116:12
What shall I render unto the LORD FOR ALL His benefits toward me?

ISAIAH 53:5
But He was wounded for our transgressions, He was bruised for our iniquities: the chastisement of our peace was upon Him; and with his stripes we are healed.

LUKE 21:34-36

And take heed to yourselves, lest at any time your hearts be overcharged with surfeiting (obesity), and drunkenness (alcohol/alcoholic), and cares of this life (P-A-R-T-Y), and so that day come upon you unawares.

For as a snares shall it come on <u>ALL them (PEOPLE) that dwell on the face of the whole earth.</u>

Watch ye therefore, and pray always, that ye may be accounted worthy to escape all these things that shall come to pass, and to stand before the Son of man.

#1 PRESCRIPTION

START HERE:

MATTHEW 22:37-38
JESUS said unto him, *THOU SHALT LOVE THE LORD THY GOD WITH ALL THY HEART, AND WITH ALL THY SOUL, AND WITH ALL THY MIND.*

This is the first and great commandment.

MATTHEW 22:39
And the second is like unto it, THOU SHALT LOVE THY NEIGHBOUR AS THYSELF.

MATTHEW 22: 40
ON THESE TWO COMMANDMENTS HANG ALL THE LAW AND THE PROPHETS

#1 PRESCRIPTION

EXODUS 20: 1-5 <u>COMMANDMENTS</u>

And GOD spoke all these words, saying:
I am the LORD your GOD, which have
brought thee out of the land of Egypt, out
of the house of bondage.

Thou shalt have no other gods before me.

Thou shalt not make unto thee any graven
image, or any likeness of anything that is
in heaven above, or that is in the earth
beneath, or that is in the water under the
earth.

Thou shalt not bow down thyself to them,
nor serve them: for I the LORD thy GOD am
a jealous GOD, visiting the iniquity of the
fathers upon the children unto the third and
fourth generation of them that hate me.

#1 PRESCRIPTION

EXODUS 20: 6-10 <u>COMMANDMENTS</u>
And shewing mercy unto thousands of them that love me, and keep my commandments.

Thou shalt not take the name of the LORD thy GOD in vain: for the LORD will not hold him guiltless that taketh his name in vain.

Remember the Sabbath day, to keep it holy.

Six days shalt thou labour, and do all thy work.

But the seventh day is the Sabbath of the LORD Thy GOD: in it thou shalt not do any work, thou, nor thy son, nor thy daughter, thy manservant, or thy maidservant, nor thy cattle, or thy stranger that is within thy gates (household).

#1 PRESCRIPTION

EXODUS 20: 11-17 <u>COMMANDMENTS</u>
For in six days the LORD made heaven and earth, the sea, and all that in them is, and rested the seventh day: wherefore the LORD blessed the Sabbath day, and hallowed it.

Honour thy father and thy mother: that thy days may be long upon the land which the LORD thy GOD giveth thee.

Thou shalt not kill

Thou shalt not commit adultery

Thou shalt not steal.

Thou shalt not bear false witness against your neighbour.

Thou shalt not covet your neighbour's house.

Thou shalt not covet your neighbour's wife,

#1 PRESCRIPTION

EXODUS 20:17-19 <u>COMMANDMENTS</u>
Thou shalt not covet your neighbour's manservant.

Thou shalt not covet your neighbour's maidservant.

Thou shalt not covet your neighbour's ox.

Thou shalt not covet your neighbour's ass, nor anything that is thy neighbour's.

And all the people saw the thunderings, and the lightnings, and the noise of the trumpet, and the mountain smoking: and when the people saw it, they removed, and stood afar off.

And they said unto Moses, Speak thou with us, and we will hear; but let not GOD speak with us, lest we die.

ROMANS 13:10-12

Love worketh no ill to his neighbour: therefore love is the fulfilling of the law.

And that, knowing the time, that now it is high time to awake out of sleep: for now is our salvation nearer than when we believed.

The night is far spent, the day is at hand: let us therefore cast off the works of darkness (Satan), and let us put on the armour of light (JESUS).

PART V
QUESTIONS

1ST TIME IN LIFE FOR A

2ND CHANCE IN LIFE

QUESTION: #1
WHAT IS MY PURPOSE ON EARTH?

ANSWER
ECCLESIASTES 12:13
Let us hear the conclusion of the whole matter: Fear GOD, and keep his commandments: for this is the whole duty of man.

QUESTION: #2
WHO CAN I TRUST?

ANSWER:
JOHN 2: 23-25
Now when He JESUS was in Jerusalem at the Passover, in the feast day, many believed in His JESUS name, when they saw the miracles which he did. But JESUS did not commit himself unto them, because he <u>KNEW ALL MEN</u>, And needed not that any should testify of man; for He <u>KNEW WHAT WAS IN MAN</u> <u>(Lucifer/Satan/Devil).</u>

<u>**ECCLESIASTES 7:20**</u>
For there is not a just man upon earth, that doeth good, and sinneth not.

ISAIAH 64:6
But <u>we are all</u> as an unclean thing, and <u>all our</u> righteousness's are as filthy rags; and <u>we all</u> do fade (die) as a leaf; and <u>our</u> iniquities, like the wind, have taken us away.

JEREMIAH 6:16
Thus saith the LORD, Stand ye in the ways, and see, and ask for the old paths, where is the good way, and walk therein, and ye shall find rest for your souls. But they said, we will not walk therein.

WARNING!

QUESTION: #3
WILL I BE PUNISHED FOR MY REBELLIOUS SPIRIT?

ANSWER:
SIN IS SIN AND NO SIN GOES UNPUNISHED

I PETER 4:16-19
JUDGMENT BEGIN AT THE HOUSE OF GOD
Yet if any man suffer as a Christian, let him not be ashamed; but let him glorify GOD on this behalf.

For the time is come that judgment must begin at the house of GOD: and if it first begin at us, what shall the end be of them that obey not the gospel of GOD?

AND IF THE RIGHTEOUS SCARCELY BE SAVED, WHERE SHALL THE UNGODLY AND THE SINNER APPEAR ?

Wherefore let them that suffer according to the will of GOD commit the keeping of their souls to him in well doing, as unto a faithful Creator.

WARNING!

2 PETER 2:4-8

For if GOD spared not the angels that sinned, but cast them down to hell, and delivered them into chains of darkness, to be reserved unto judgment.

And spared not the old world, but saved Noah the eighth person, a preacher of righteousness, bringing in the flood upon the <u>world of the ungodly.</u>

And turning the cities of Sodom and Gomorrah into ashes condemned them with an overthrow, making them an example unto those that after should <u>live ungodly.</u>

And delivered just Lot, vexed with the filthy conversation of the wicked. (For the righteous man dwelling among them, in seeing and hearing, vexed his righteous soul from day to day with their unlawful deeds);

WARNING!

QUESTION: #4

WILL I BE PUNISHED IF I DO NOT BELIEVE IN GOD ONLY BEGOTTEN SON NAME?

ANSWER:
THE WORD OF GOD IN THE HOLY BIBLE SAY

JOHN 3:17-18 CONDEMNATION

For GOD sent <u>not</u> his Son into the world to condemn the world (people); but that the world (people) through him might be saved.

He that believeth on him JESUS is not condemned; <u>but he that believeth not is condemned already,</u> because he hath not believed in the name of the only begotten Son of GOD.

1CORINTHIANS 3:16

TEMPLE OF GOD IN ME

Know ye not that ye are the temple of GOD, and that the Spirit of GOD dwelleth in you?

If any man defile the temple of GOD, Him shall GOD destroy (kill); for the temple of GOD is holy, which temple ye are.

QUESTION: #5

WHAT SHALL I DO NOW?

JOSHUA 24:15
CHOOSE YE THIS DAY

And if it seem evil unto you to serve the LORD, choose you this day whom ye will serve: whether the gods which your fathers served that were on the other side of the flood, or the gods of the Amorites, in whose land ye dwell: but as for me and my house, we will serve the LORD..

2 TIMOTHY 4:5   WATCH AND PRAY

But **watch** thou in all things, endure afflictions, do the work of an evangelist, make full proof of thy ministry.

MATTHEW 26:41 -*Watch and pray, that ye enter not into temptation: the spirit indeed is willing, but the flesh is weak.*

MARK 13:33-34 -*Take heed,* **watch** *and pray: for ye know not when the time is. For the Son of man is as a man taking a far journey, who left his house, and gave authority to his servants, and to every man his work, and commanded the porter to watch.*

MARK 13:35 -*Watch ye therefore: for ye know not when the master of the house cometh, <u>at even</u>, or <u>at midnight</u>, or <u>at the cockcrowing</u>, or <u>in the morning</u>.*

1 CORINTHIANS 16:13-14 – **Watch** ye, stand fast in the faith, quit you like men, be strong. Let all your things be done with LOVE.

I THESSALONIANS 5:4-6 –But ye, brethren, are not in darkness, that that day should overtake you as a thief.

I THESSALONIANS 5:5 -Ye are all the children of LIGHT, and the children of the DAY: we are not of the night, nor of darkness.

I THESSALONIANS 5:6 -Therefore **<u>let us not SLEEP</u>**, as do others; but let us **WATCH** and be **SOBER**.

HEBREWS 13:17 –Obey them that have the rule over you, and submit yourselves: for they **watch** for your souls, as they that must give account, that they may do it with joy, and not with grief: for that is unprofitable for you.

1 PETER 4:7 –But the end of all thins is at hand: be ye therefore **SOBER**, and **WATCH** unto prayer.

1 PETER 4:8 –And above all things have fervent LOVE among yourselves: for LOVE SHALL COVER THE MULTITUDE OF SINS.

REVELATION 3:3 –*Remember therefore how thou hast received and heard, and hold fast and repent. **If therefore thou shalt NOT WATCH**, I will come on thee as a thief, and thou shalt not know what hour I will come upon thee.*

QUESTION: #6

DID JESUS COME TO BRING PEACE ON EARTH?

ANSWER:
THE WORD OF GOD IN THE HOLY BIBLE SAY:

MATTHEW 10: 34-35-36
Think not that I JESUS am come to send <u>PEACE</u> on earth: I came not to send PEACE, but a <u>SWORD</u>.

For I JESUS am come to set a man at variance <u>against</u> his father, and the daughter <u>against</u> her mother, and the daughter-in-law <u>against</u> her mother-in-law.

And a man's foe <u>(ENEMIES)</u> (husband/ children /wife) shall be they of his own household.

PROVERBS 25:17
Withdraw thy foot from they neighbor's house; lest he be weary of thee, and so hate thee.

MARK 10:6-9

But from the beginning of the creation GOD made them male and female. For this cause shall a MAN (uncles/ nephews/ brothers, grandsons) *LEAVE his father and mother* (house/shelter etc.,) *and CLEAVE to his wife* (not grandmother/ grandfather/ mother/ sister/aunt, etc.) (for better or worst) *and they twain (2) shall be one (1) flesh: so then they are <u>no more twain (2),</u> but one (1) flesh* (same spirit).

What therefore GOD hath joined together, let not man put asunder (uncles/ nephews/ brothers / sisters aunts/ grandmother/ grandfather / father/mother/ sister/aunt/ homosexuals, perverts, peepers , bi-sexual etc.,)

JUDE 1:24-25

Now unto him that is able to keep you from falling, and to present you faultless before the presence of his glory with exceeding joy.

To the only wise GOD our Saviour, be glory and majesty, dominion and power, both now and ever. Amen.

NOW

IF YOU ARE NEARING 50 YEARS OF AGE OR 50 NOW. AND YOU HAVE NOT THE KNOWLEDGE OF THE HOLY. READ THE BOOK NICODEMUS BORN AGAIN IN THE 90'S.

AND PRAY TO JESUS FOR A REVELATION OF YOUR READING.

PLEASE DO NOT LOOK AT HILDA'S FAULTS AND SHORT COMINGS IN THIS BOOK. GET YOUR OWN HOUSE IN ORDER (INSIDE YOUR BODY).

NICODEMUS IS A NO BODY TRYING TO TELL EVERYBODY TO TASTE AND SEE THAT THE LORD IS GOOD.

NEXT

YOU FEEL YOU CANNOT CAUGHT THE VISION OF JESUS MINISTRY WORK AFTER READING THE BOOK NICODEMUS BORN AGAIN IN THE 90's.

<u>NEXT</u>
QUESTION: DO YOU SAY AND I QUOTE" I JUST WANT TO P-A-R-T-Y.

IF YOUR ANSWER IS YES.

LUCFIER/SATAN/DEVIL HAS SEEN GOD FACE. WE HAVE NOT.

DO NOT PARTAKE IN (LUCIFIER/ SATAN/DEVIL) ACITVITIES.

I PRAY THAT WE GET OUR HOUSE IN OUR BODY IN ORDER.

REVELATION 22:10-13

And he saith unto me, Seal not the sayings of the prophecy of this book: for the time is at hand.

He that is **UNJUST**, let him be **UNJUST** still:

and he which is **FILTHY**, let him be **FILTHY** still:

and he that is **RIGHTEOUS**, let him be **RIGHTEOUS** still:

and he that is **HOLY**, let him be **HOLY** still.

*And, behold, I **JESUS** come quickly; and my reward is with me, to give every man according as his work shall be.*

*I am **ALPHA** and **OMEGA**, the beginning and the end, the first and the last.*

ISAIAH 40:31

BUT THEY THAT WAIT UPON THE LORD SHALL RENEW THEIR STRENGTH; THEY SHALL MOUNT UP WITH WINGS AS EAGLES; THEY SHALL RUN, AND NOT BE WEARY; AND THEY SHALL WALK, AND NOT FAINT.

1 PETER 2:25
FOR YE WERE AS SHEEP GOING ASTRAY;
but are now returned unto the Shepherd
(pastor) and Bishop of your soul.

JESUS THE HIGH PRIEST.
GOD ONLY BEGOTTEN SON.
JESUS IS LORD. AMEN.